W9-COY-781

ILLINOIS

Past and Present

Joanne Mattern

rosen publishing's
rosen
central

New York

For my family

Published in 2010 by The Rosen Publishing Group, Inc.
29 East 21st Street, New York, NY 10010

Library of Congress Cataloging-in-Publication Data

Mattern, Joanne, 1963–
Illinois: past and present / Joanne Mattern.—1st ed.
    p. cm.—(The United States: past and present)
Includes bibliographical references and index.
ISBN-13: 978-1-4358-5284-6 (library binding)
ISBN-13: 978-1-4358-5566-3 (pbk)
ISBN-13: 978-1-4358-5567-0 (6 pack)
1. Illinois—Juvenile literature. I. Title.
F541.3.M386 2010
977.3—dc22

2008050577

Manufactured in the United States of America

On the cover: Top left: When Chicago hosted the World's Fair in 1893, it marked the rebirth of a city that had been destroyed by fire twenty-two years earlier. Top right: Customers enjoy the bounty of an Illinois pumpkin harvest. Illinois is one of the top pumpkin producers in the United States. Bottom: Chicago is the largest city in Illinois and a center of commerce and industry for the nation.

Contents

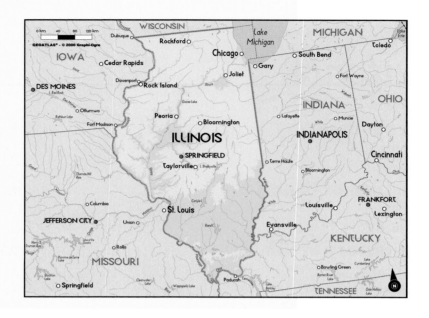

Illinois's central location—and the fact that it borders both Lake Michigan and the Mississippi River—has given the state an important role in our nation's history.

Introduction

Illinois has many nicknames. It is known as the "Land of Lincoln" because of its most famous resident, President Abraham Lincoln. The state is also called the "Prairie State" because of the vast grasslands that once made up most of its land. As these nicknames show, Illinois is a place of history, tradition, and beauty. Although it has never boasted the largest population or the biggest area of the states, Illinois is one of the most important places in American geography and history.

When you look at a map and see how Illinois borders the southern part of Lake Michigan on one side and the mighty Mississippi River on the other, it's easy to understand why Illinois became such a powerful center of industry and business. In the early days of Illinois's history, water was the major way to transport goods and people. Lake Michigan, along with rivers and a canal system, made it easy to transport goods from east to west and back again. Hogs and cattle from the Southwest and Midwest traveled through Illinois on their way to markets in the East. Lumber traveled from the eastern forests through Illinois to build new cities and towns.

Illinois has changed greatly over the years. What started as a grassy, open area of Native American settlements changed into rolling fields of corn and soybeans and then into crowded cities and towns. Through it all, the people of Illinois have held on to a pioneer spirit and the awareness that their state is large in history and industry, if not in size. Let's turn the page and see all that Illinois has to offer.

THE LAND OF ILLINOIS

Illinois is the twenty-fifth largest state in the United States, placing it in the middle of the fifty states in size. The total area of Illinois is 57,915 square miles (149,999 square kilometers). Most of the state is flat or covered by gently rolling hills. The Mississippi River creates the western border of the state, while Lake Michigan lies to the northeast. Illinois is about 385 miles (620 km) long and about 218 miles (351 km) wide.

Geography

Geographers have divided the state into several areas. These areas contain a variety of landforms and are home to a huge number of plants and animals.

The northwest corner of Illinois is called the Driftless Area. Thousands of years ago, this area was covered by glaciers. The glaciers created deep valleys and rugged hills. Charles Mound, the highest point in the state, is found in the Driftless Area.

The Central Plains make up about 90 percent of the state. Part of the Central Plains is called the Great Lakes Plain. It is found along Lake Michigan, and millions of years ago, it was actually part of the

The prairies that once covered Illinois are long gone, but parts of them remain. Here in the Middle Fork State Fish and Wildlife Area, a horse trail curves through the fall grassland.

lake. The Till Plains are the largest section of the Central Plains. The Till Plains have very fertile soil. This soil helped Illinois become one of the leading agricultural states in the nation.

The Shawnee Hills are located south of the Central Plains. This narrow area covers a strip of land in the southern part of Illinois. As you might guess from its name, the Shawnee Hills area is covered by steep hills and deep valleys.

The extreme southern tip of Illinois, known as the Gulf Coastal Plain, is different from any other part of the state. The land here has

The Mississippi and Ohio rivers are two important bodies of water in Illinois. Here, the two mighty rivers meet at the southern border of the state.

gentle hills and many swamps. The area is so wet that parts of it look like the swampy areas found in the southeastern United States.

Illinois has several major rivers and lakes. The largest and most important river is the Mississippi. This river runs along the western edge of Illinois. Other major rivers include the Illinois River, which flows from Chicago through the center of the state; the Ohio River, which flows across the southern tip of the state; and the Wabash River in the southeastern corner of Illinois. Lake Michigan is the largest of Illinois's lakes. It is located in the upper northeast corner of the state. Another important body of water is Rend Lake in the southern part of the state.

Climate

Illinois has a temperate climate, which means the climate is not extremely hot or extremely cold. Winters in Illinois are cold and snowy, while summers are usually hot and wet. The temperate climate makes it possible for Illinois to be a suitable home for a variety of animals and plants.

Illinois's woods are home to a variety of animals, both large and small. These white-tailed deer are among the largest animals in the state and live throughout the area.

Animal Life

Many animals call Illinois home. More than five hundred different species of mammals, birds, and fish live in the state, along with about one hundred species of reptiles and amphibians.

White-tailed deer are among the largest animals in Illinois. Other common mammals include bobcats, muskrats, beavers, foxes, minks, squirrels, otters, raccoons, and skunks. Large populations of bats live in caves, especially in the southern part of the state.

The Prairie

Several hundred years ago, Illinois was covered by the prairie. Rolling grasslands stretched as far as the eye could see in every direction. The land was covered with a variety of tall grasses and wildflowers. Small animals, such as rabbits, snakes, and ground birds, made their homes in the thick cover of grass.

Today, a person looking across the landscape is likely to see vast fields of corn or soybeans, not prairie grasses and flowers. Illinois government officials and many residents want to save the prairie. The government is working to reintroduce native wildflowers and grasses that were plowed up long ago, and it encourages residents to plant prairie gardens featuring native plants. The government has also set aside nature preserves to show the land's natural state. Although Illinois will never again be covered by rolling expanses of prairie, it is important to preserve the natural landscape. These protected areas are small compared to the vast lands the prairie used to cover, but they give a hint of what the area used to look like.

There are also many birds in the state. Large populations of Canada geese and ducks live in Illinois. Snow geese and blue geese spend winters in the state, when the areas to the north are too cold. Bald eagles and golden eagles are also found in Illinois, along with smaller species, such as cardinals, blue jays, and owls.

Illinois's lakes, streams, and rivers provide a home to a wide variety of fish. Common fish include sunfish, trout, bluegill, bass, and catfish.

Reptiles—such as snakes, turtles, and small lizards—also live in Illinois, as do frogs, toads, salamanders, and other amphibians. All of these animals are able to find good habitats in Illinois's plains and forests.

A variety of colorful wildflowers grow on the prairie. In Goose Lake Prairie State Park, two brightly colored flowers called prairie blazing stars stand out in a field of yellow goldenrod.

Plant Life

At one time, Illinois was covered with prairie. Prairies are large areas of rolling grasslands, with very few trees, but with many different types of grasses and flowers. As more and more settlers came to the area, much of the prairie disappeared. People plowed the grasslands and transformed the rich earth into farmland instead.

Today, however, there are still more than 2,500 native plant species in Illinois. The state boasts a wide variety of flowers, including black-eyed Susans, violets, and sunflowers, as well as clover and wild onions.

The state's trees include oak, sugar maple, beech, ash, hickory, walnut, peach, and apple. The swampy Gulf Coastal Plain is home to bald cypress and tupelo gum trees, which are usually found only in the Deep South.

Chapter 2

THE HISTORY OF ILLINOIS

Illinois is centrally located in North America, and its rolling plains and plentiful water supply have made it an appealing home for a variety of different groups. All of these groups changed Illinois and brought it into the center of many historical and cultural events.

Native American Settlers

Illinois's first residents were Native Americans. The first group of Native Americans to reside in the area, called the Paleo-Indians, arrived about ten thousand years ago. They lived in forests and caves and hunted large animals. Not much is known about these Native Americans or why they disappeared.

The Mound Builders

Between 1000 BCE and 1600 CE, other Native Americans settled in the area. They built settlements and farmed. They also made pottery. Because these Native Americans buried their dead in earth mounds, they became known as the Mound Builders. The Mound Builders were one of the most advanced Native American cultures in North America. They created works of art, used science to study the universe, and established trade routes. These trade

Cahokia Mounds State Historic Site is the largest prehistoric site north of Mexico. It is a fascinating place to visit and see an ancient way of life.

routes stretched from the Great Lakes all the way south to the Gulf of Mexico.

The Mound Builders also founded a city called Cahokia in the southwestern part of Illinois, near today's border with the state of Missouri. In 1050, as many as thirty thousand people lived in Cahokia. Today, the remains of Cahokia can be seen at the Cahokia Mounds State Historic Site.

During the 1200s, the Mound Builders' culture began to die out. These Native Americans may have disappeared because of poor food, overcrowding, or an outbreak of disease. By 1500, the Mound Builders were all gone.

French missionary Louis Nicolas drew this sketch of a Native American chief around the year 1701.

The Illiniwek

It did not take long for another Native American group to take control of the area. This group was called the Illini or the Illiniwek, which means "the people." The state of Illinois is named after them. The Illiniwek lived in villages for most of the year. They planted corn and other crops. During the rest of the year, the Illiniwek traveled over the plains to hunt buffalo. The Illiniwek were part of the Algonquian nation and formed the largest Native American tribe in the area. By the 1670s, there were about ten thousand Illiniwek living in Illinois.

Later, Iroquois tribes moved into the Midwest and became an important nation as well. However, Illinois was about to see new settlers. These people had come all the way from Europe.

The Europeans Arrive

The first Europeans to arrive in Illinois were two French explorers named Jacques Marquette and Louis Jolliet. They arrived in 1673, traveling along the Mississippi River and the Illinois River. Marquette and Jolliet had lived in Canada, which was then a French colony. They were able to communicate with the Illiniwek and had a friendly relationship with them.

Marquette and Jolliet's explorations helped open Illinois and the Midwest to French traders from Canada and Europe. Most of these traders were interested in obtaining animal furs. At the time, there was a huge market for furs to be made into clothing, hats, and other articles. It did not take long before many French fur traders came to Illinois to hunt, trap, and trade with the Native Americans. The traders introduced many aspects of European culture to the Illiniwek.

French missionary and explorer Jacques Marquette was one of the first Europeans to visit Illinois. He traveled down the Mississippi River and met many Native Americans.

Missionaries were another group of settlers. Instead of being interested in fur trading, these men were interested in religion. They lived and traveled among the Native Americans, teaching them about Christianity. Slowly, many of the Native Americans' religious customs disappeared.

The arrival of the Europeans had a profound influence on Native American life. Not only did the Native Americans accept European culture and religion, but they also fell victim to European diseases. Fur traders and missionaries brought deadly diseases into the area, and the Native Americans had no resistance to them. Thousands died from smallpox, measles, plague, and other diseases.

As the Native American population got smaller, France was able to take control of Illinois. In 1671, the French claimed the area as part of their own territory. They built forts, trading posts, and towns. However, the French were not the only Europeans in the area. The British had also arrived. Once again, Illinois was going to change dramatically.

The British Are Coming!

The late 1600s saw the arrival of large numbers of British traders and settlers. Like the French, the British were looking for furs and other items to trade and sell. It didn't take long for the French and British to become bitter enemies as they fought over territory and trading rights.

From 1754 to 1763, the French and British fought each other in the French and Indian War. Most Native Americans fought on the side of the French. However, the British won the war. The war officially ended with the Treaty of Paris. This treaty gave all the land east of the Mississippi River to the British. Illinois was now under British control.

The arrival of the British meant the end of the Native Americans' society in Illinois. Between 1700 and 1750, the Native American population of Illinois dropped from six thousand to one thousand. By the time the British won control of the area, almost all of the Native Americans had left Illinois.

Statehood and Beyond

The British did not keep control of Illinois for long. Between 1776 and 1783, the thirteen British colonies on the eastern coast fought against

In 1874, Chicago was already rebuilding from a devastating fire just three years earlier. The city's location on Lake Michigan made it a natural center of transportation and commerce.

Great Britain in the American Revolution. After winning their freedom, the colonies and the other British territories in North America became the new country of the United States of America. In 1818, the territory of Illinois became the twenty-first state in the nation. Illinois's population of just thirty-five thousand people made it the smallest state. However, Illinois was about to experience new growth.

As the population of the United States grew, settlers moved west in search of more land and better opportunities. Illinois was in the perfect location to benefit from this westward migration. Many settlers were happy to make new homes in Illinois, and they soon

Rebuilding Chicago

In 1871, Chicago was a crowded, prosperous city. On the night of October 8, disaster struck. A fire started in a barn and spread quickly through the city's wooden buildings. The blaze was so hot and fierce that one fireman called the blaze "the devil's own fire." It wasn't until a rainstorm on October 10 that the fire finally died out. Stunned residents were left with complete devastation: 300 people killed, 100,000 people homeless, and property worth $200 million destroyed. Many people believed Chicago would never rise from the ashes.

However, a building boom began immediately, and Chicago soon regained its place as one of America's largest and most important cities. Today, Chicago is one of the country's financial and industrial centers. Many corporations, banks, and factories are located there, and the city is a thriving home to millions of people. The city's skyline gleams with shining skyscrapers, and its streets are filled with people hurrying to work in a variety of businesses and trades. Almost three million people call Chicago home, making it the third-largest city in the United States.

transformed the prairie into farmland. New inventions, such as John Deere's steel plow blade, helped to make plowing the land easier. This led to even more people moving to Illinois. By 1830, the state's population had grown to 150,000.

More people came during the next fifty years. Canals—and later, railroads—made it easier to travel to the area. Along with settlers from the eastern United States, many immigrants flocked to Illinois. These immigrants came from all over Europe, including Ireland, Germany, Poland, Russia, Italy, and Greece. Many people went to work in the mines or in the new factories that were springing up all

Chicago's night sky blazes with light from its many tall buildings. The Sears Tower, at left, is the tallest building in the city.

over the state. Others worked on the farms that were still a major resource in the state.

Modern Illinois

Illinois continued to grow and prosper during the 1900s and into the 2000s. Illinois is still an important crop-producing state, and it is also a center of industry and transportation. Over the years, job opportunities have opened the state to new waves of settlers and immigrants, including African Americans, Latinos, and Asians.

Chicago is Illinois's largest city and has always been an important center of trade and culture. The city began as a simple trading cabin. By 1870, its population had swelled to 300,000. Chicago's growth came because of its excellent location. Since the city was on the shores of Lake Michigan, it was easy to ship goods to the East. Chicago's central location made it a natural shipping point to the West as well. Today, Chicago is a major industrial, financial, and cultural center.

Chapter 3

THE GOVERNMENT OF ILLINOIS

Like the United States, Illinois is governed by a set of rules called a constitution. The state constitution lists the most important rights and laws for residents of the state. It also lists the powers of each branch of the state government.

Illinois's government is divided into three parts: the executive branch, the legislative branch, and the judicial branch. Illinois set up its state government just like the federal government, with a three-branch system. This system helps to ensure fairness because no one branch can gain too much power.

The government of Illinois is based in the state capital, Springfield. Government institutions located in Springfield include the office of the governor, the Illinois General Assembly, and the Illinois Supreme Court.

The Executive Branch

The executive branch makes sure that the laws are enforced. In the federal government, the president is the head of the executive branch. Similarly, the governor is the head of the state executive branch. There are several other people who make up Illinois's executive branch: the lieutenant governor, the attorney general, the comptroller, the treasurer,

The capitol building stands tall in Illinois's capital city, Springfield. Springfield became the state's capital in 1837.

and the secretary of state. All of these officers are elected by the people every four years.

The governor is the head of the state's government. The governor prepares the state's budget, appoints managers, approves or rejects bills (drafts of new laws), and oversees the state's military. The lieutenant governor is the governor's second-in-command. He or she is just like the vice president of the United States—ready to help the leader and to take over any responsibilities if necessary. The lieutenant governor runs several committees.

The secretary of state oversees many different departments of the government, including those dealing with voting rights, driving privileges, and other aspects of daily life. Illinois's secretary of state is a busy person because this official has more duties than the secretary of state in any other state.

The attorney general works closely with the courts. His or her job is to make sure that the state's court system and the Department of Justice run smoothly. He or she also serves as the state's lawyer in major court cases and other legal issues.

The comptroller and the treasurer are both involved in the state's finances. The treasurer controls the money and the state budget. The comptroller—the state's accountant—makes sure that the financial process runs smoothly and that the state's expenses do not get too high.

The Legislative Branch

The role of the legislative branch is to make new laws. In the U.S. government, the legislature is made up of the House of Representatives and the Senate. Both houses include members from every state so that all parts of the United States are represented. In Illinois, the legislature is also made up of two houses, which include representatives from all parts of the state.

In Illinois, the legislative branch is called the General Assembly. Its two houses are called the Senate and the House of Representatives. The Senate has fifty-nine members. Each member represents a large area of the state. These state senators are elected every four years. The House of Representatives has 118 members. Each member represents a smaller area of the state than the senators do. In fact, a member

The Chicago Machine

Richard J. Daley and his son, Richard M. Daley, have dominated Chicago's politics for more than fifty years.

In addition to the state government, Illinois has many local governments. One of the most powerful local governments is found in the city of Chicago. Chicago's government oversees a huge number of agencies and projects.

From 1955 to 1976, Richard J. Daley was mayor of Chicago. Daley was so powerful that his government became known as the "Chicago Machine." Daley gave out jobs in exchange for votes. Some said he ruled more like a dictator than a democratically elected official. Citizens were told how to vote and were threatened with a loss of benefits if they did not comply. Daley's rules may have been unfair, but he got things done. Under his leadership, Chicago built new housing and improved its transportation systems. He became one of the most famous mayors in U.S. history, and his influence extended from Illinois all the way to the federal government. Presidential candidates knew that if they had Daley on their side, he could guarantee millions of votes.

Today, there is another Daley in charge of Chicago. Richard J. Daley's son, Richard M. Daley, has been the mayor of Chicago since 1989. In 2007, he was re-elected with more than 70 percent of the vote. The younger Daley has achieved national attention. In 2005, *Time* magazine named him one of the best mayors in the nation. Daley's accomplishments include a more diverse city workforce and increased funding for the arts. Although Richard M. Daley is powerful and influential and not afraid to do things his way, the Chicago Machine is a thing of the past.

might represent just a few towns or part of a larger city. Elections for the House of Representatives are held every two years.

The two houses work together to create new laws. Any member of the General Assembly can sponsor a bill that he or she would like to become a new state law. Then, different committees work on the bill to create a version that most members can agree with. Some bills are rejected or changed quite a bit, while others are accepted. Once a bill is accepted, members of the House or the Senate vote on the bill, depending on which house the sponsoring member came from. If one house accepts the bill, it moves to the other house for another

Illinois's state senators meet in the Senate Chamber in Springfield to draft new laws.

vote. Finally, if both houses pass the bill, it moves on to the governor. The governor may veto, or reject, the bill or may sign the bill into law. The legislature can also vote to change a law that is already on the books.

The Judicial Branch

The judicial branch of government interprets the laws. Illinois's judicial branch includes more than 750 judges. About four hundred of those judges are elected by the state's residents. The governor appoints the other 350 judges.

The bottom rung of the court system is made up of the county circuit courts. There are twenty-two judicial circuits in the state. If a person is arrested, he or she appears in one of these courts for trial and sentencing.

Sometimes, people do not agree with the rulings of a circuit court. When that happens, the person can appeal his or her case to an appellate court. In an appeal, a person or group takes a lower court's decision to this higher court for review. Sometimes, the higher court reverses or changes the decision. Illinois has five appellate court districts.

The supreme court is the highest court in the state. The Illinois Supreme Court is made up of seven judges. These judges hear cases that have already been appealed in an appellate court. These cases must be ones that challenge state laws. The judges decide if these laws violate the state's constitution. If they decide a law does violate the constitution, that law will be taken off the books or rewritten in order to be fair. In general, the decision of the supreme court is final. There is no court left in the state to which one can appeal, although some cases might be appealed in federal court.

Chapter 4

THE INDUSTRIES OF ILLINOIS

Illinois has a varied economy. The many different industries and natural and human resources have helped Illinois remain strong in the face of difficult economic changes.

Agriculture

In its early days, Illinois's major industry was farming. Today, agriculture is still one of the main industries in the state. Farmland covers nearly 80 percent of the state's landscape. The state's rich soil produces corn, soybeans, wheat, hay, and pumpkins, and Illinois is a top producer of many of these crops. Many of Illinois's crops are grown on huge "factory farms," which include millions of acres of land and use high-tech machinery and practices to produce the most food possible. This food is consumed in the United States and is also exported to countries around the world.

Illinois produces more than just crops. Its land also supports a variety of livestock, including hogs, beef and dairy cattle, chickens, and sheep. Hogs are the most popular livestock in Illinois, and the state's farmers raise hundreds of thousands of these animals every year. Many of Illinois's animals are raised and sold for their meat or to produce milk, cheese, or eggs for people to eat.

The Caterpillar factory in Peoria is one of the world's major manufacturers of construction equipment. This photo shows a section of the original factory with its antique machinery.

Manufacturing

Manufacturing has been an important industry in Illinois for almost two hundred years. During the 1800s, John Deere and Cyrus McCormick revolutionized farming with their inventions that made it easier to plow fields and harvest crops. They and other manufacturers of farming equipment set up operations in the area. During the twentieth century, the Caterpillar factory in Peoria became one of the world's major manufacturers of tractors, bull-dozers, and other construction equipment. In 2001, Chicago received

Mining Towns

In 1811, the first coal mines opened in Illinois. These mines became the lifeblood of many towns in the southern part of the state. Workers flocked to the mines, even though the work was backbreaking, dangerous, and often deadly. Miners' families filled the houses in the factory towns, and miners' paychecks kept many businesses open. The mines employed thousands of people and used machinery manufactured and repaired by Illinois factories.

By the 1990s, all of that had changed. Coal supplies were depleted. Mines closed, throwing thousands of people out of work. Stores and other businesses in mining towns closed, and people moved out of some communities in search of jobs elsewhere.

Today, Illinois's residents and government officials are working hard to improve the economy. Abandoned buildings are being torn down and replaced by high-tech businesses. Some communities are relying more on tourism, building museums and promoting local historical or natural sites to draw more people to the area. Other communities are encouraging foreign companies to open factories in the state. Like other parts of the country, Illinois is working hard to find new ways to survive and thrive.

a major financial boost when aircraft manufacturer Boeing moved its world headquarters to the city.

Illinois has factories that produce a variety of products, including machinery, computers, electrical equipment, chemicals, and steel. Food processing is another major manufacturing industry, as factories process much of the food that is raised in Illinois's fertile fields, including crops and meat.

Mining

Underground, Illinois is full of natural resources. The state produces the nation's largest variety of minerals, including lead, zinc, fluorite, coal, and oil. Most mines are found in the southern part of the state, near the cities of East St. Louis, Carbondale (which was named for its deposits of coal), and Champaign. Peat, stone, clay, and gravel are also mined in Illinois.

The city of Galena once produced 85 percent of the lead in the United States. Although production has fallen in recent years, lead and zinc are still mined in the area. Illinois also produces the most fluorite in the world. This mineral is used to make steel, glass, and chemicals.

Chicago's O'Hare Airport is the second-busiest airport in the world. It is named after a famous World War II pilot, Edward "Butch" O'Hare.

Transportation

Because of its key location on Lake Michigan, Chicago has been a leading transportation center since the pioneer days. Goods are still shipped by boat, train, and trucks through the city. As in the past, the city is a center of shipping, train, and air routes. Chicago's huge O'Hare Airport is one of the busiest airports in the world, handling more than 160,000 passengers every day.

A trader on the floor of the Chicago Mercantile Exchange works a stock trade. Chicago is an important financial center.

Big Business

Chicago is the financial capital of the Midwest. It has its own stock exchange, along with a huge banking industry. Many more banks and financial companies are located in other parts of the state as well. Several major insurance companies are located in Illinois, including State Farm and Allstate.

You've probably heard of the companies Kraft, Sara Lee, Walgreen's, Sears, Motorola, and Quaker Oats. All of these major companies have their headquarters in Illinois. So does McDonald's.

Service

Tourism is an important part of Illinois's economy. The observation deck of the Sears Tower provides tourists a panoramic view of Chicago.

Service workers make up three-quarters of the jobs in Illinois. The service industry includes many different jobs. A service worker can be employed by the government, the school system, hospitals, insurance companies, or banks.

Tourism is another important part of the economy, both in Chicago and throughout the state. Service workers work in stores, hotels, restaurants, entertainment centers, and media outlets, all of which rely on tourists for a large part of their income.

Illinois's excellent geographic location—as well as its strengths in natural and human resources—make it likely that the state will continue to thrive in the years to come.

Chapter 5

PEOPLE FROM ILLINOIS: PAST AND PRESENT

Illinois is the birthplace or home of many Americans who have made a difference in the world. Let's meet some of Illinois's most famous citizens.

Jane Addams (1860–1935) Addams was born in Cedarville in 1860. She dedicated her life to social activism, helping the poor immigrants who flooded into Chicago during the late 1800s. She opened Hull House, a settlement house that aided immigrants, the poor, and their children, and she also worked to establish juvenile courts. In 1931, Addams became the first American woman to win the Nobel Peace Prize.

Ray Bradbury (1920–) Bradbury was born in Waukegan in 1920. He is a well-known author of science fiction and fantasy who has won many awards. Bradbury's most famous novels include *Fahrenheit 451* and *The Martian Chronicles*.

Sandra Cisneros (1954–) Cisneros was born to a Mexican American family in Chicago and grew up speaking Spanish. One of the most famous Latina authors in the world, she has

Born and raised in Illinois, Hillary Rodham Clinton became the U.S. Secretary of State in 2009.

set many of her stories in Chicago. Cisneros is best known for her award-winning novel *The House on Mango Street*.

Hillary Rodham Clinton (1947–) Hillary Rodham Clinton was born in Chicago and grew up in the suburb of Park Ridge. She worked as a lawyer and children's rights advocate, and she was first lady of the United States during her husband Bill Clinton's presidency from 1993 to 2001. Later, she became a U.S. senator for the state of New York. In 2008, she ran for president but lost the Democratic nomination to another politician from Illinois, Barack Obama. Shortly after his win, Obama appointed Clinton to serve as Secretary of State. She was confirmed in January 2009.

Walt Disney (1901–1966) Disney was born in Chicago in 1901, although he moved out of the state as a child. Later, Disney returned to Chicago to study art and went on to an amazing career in animation. Disney created the characters Mickey Mouse and Donald Duck, founded Walt Disney Studios, and opened Disneyland and Walt Disney World, America's first theme parks.

Ulysses S. Grant (1822–1885) Born in Ohio in 1822, Grant lived in Galena as an adult. He served as a general in the Civil War and his heroic deeds made him so popular that he went on to serve as president of the United States from 1869 to 1877.

Mae Jemison (1956–) Jemison was born in Alabama but moved to Chicago when she was three years old. She earned several degrees, including a degree in medicine. She became the first female African American astronaut when she flew on the space shuttle *Endeavor* in 1992. After she retired from the space program, Jemison started her own technology company and worked to improve educational opportunities for children around the world.

Mae Jemison grew up in Chicago and became the first female African American astronaut in 1992.

Quincy Jones (1933–) Musician Quincy Jones was born in Chicago in 1933. He has composed jazz and popular music as well as television and movie theme songs, and he has produced best-selling music albums, such as Michael Jackson's classic *Thriller*. Jones has won more than a dozen Grammy Awards.

Michael Jordan became one of the most legendary athletes in professional sports when he led the Chicago Bulls to six championships during the 1990s.

Michael Jordan (1963–) Although he grew up in North Carolina, Jordan became famous as the center for the Chicago Bulls basketball team. Jordan is known as "His Airness" and "Air Jordan" for his ability to float through the air and sink baskets. He led the Bulls to NBA championships in 1991, 1992, 1993, 1996, 1997, and 1998.

Jackie Joyner-Kersee (1962–) Joyner-Kersee was born in East St. Louis in 1962. She became famous as a track star at UCLA and went on to win six Olympic medals in track and field. She was the first athlete to score more than seven thousand points in the heptathlon.

Ray Kroc (1902–1984) Kroc was born in Chicago in 1902. During the 1950s, he got the idea for a restaurant that served hamburgers, fries, and milkshakes from two brothers named the McDonalds. Kroc opened the first McDonald's restaurant in Des Plaines in 1955. Today, McDonald's is the most popular fast-food restaurant in the world. Kroc died in 1984.

Bill Murray (1950–) Murray was born in Wilmette in 1950 and became well-known as a comedian at Chicago's legendary

Second City comedy club. He later appeared on *Saturday Night Live* and went on to a long career in such classic movies as *Caddyshack*, *Groundhog Day*, *Ghostbusters*, and *Lost in Translation*.

Richard Peck (1934–) Peck was born in Decatur in 1934 and grew up there. He is an award-winning author of young adult books, many of which are set in Illinois. In 2001, he won the Newbery Medal for *A Year Down Yonder*.

Ronald Reagan (1911–2004) Reagan was born in Tampico and grew up in Dixon. After college, Reagan moved to California to purse an acting career. He appeared in a number of movies and then became active in Republican politics. Reagan became governor of California in 1967 and served as president of the United States from 1981 to 1989. President Reagan was a key figure in bringing about the fall of communism in the Soviet-controlled countries of Russia and Eastern Europe.

Carl Sandburg (1878–1967) This famous poet was born in 1878 in Galesburg. He lived most of his life in Chicago, where he became famous for his poetry about ordinary people in the Midwest. Sandburg also wrote a six-volume biography on Abraham Lincoln. His most famous poem, "Chicago," gave the city its nickname, "City of Big Shoulders."

Kanye West (1977–) Musician Kanye West was born in 1977 and moved to Chicago when he was three years old. His albums, such as *Late Registration* (2005) and *Graduation*

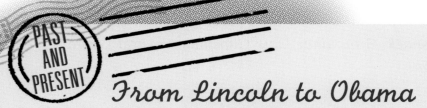

From Lincoln to Obama

Illinois has boasted connections to our nation's leaders throughout its history. Born in Kentucky in 1809, **Abraham Lincoln** and his family moved to Illinois in 1830. Lincoln became well-known as a lawyer and politician in Springfield and eventually became the sixteenth president of the United States. Lincoln was president during the Civil War, one of the most difficult periods in American history. He was instrumental in freeing the slaves and was working toward reuniting the nation when he was assassinated in 1865. Many who study history consider Lincoln to be the greatest president the United States has ever had.

In 2008—143 years later—Illinois again made presidential history when **Barack Obama** was elected the first African American president of the United States. Born in Hawaii in 1961 and raised there and in Indonesia, Obama came to Chicago to work as a lawyer and as an advocate for disadvantaged communities. His community work led him into politics, and he served in the Illinois state legislature. In 2004, he was elected U.S. senator representing Illinois. In 2008, Obama became the first African American candidate to be the Democratic party's nominee for president and to win the presidency.

Barack Obama has cited Lincoln's life and accomplishments as inspirations. He has read Lincoln's writings to help him with the difficult decisions that he faces as president. Obama's election gave hope to many people that the racial divisions that have always been part of U.S. history may finally be coming to an end.

Abraham Lincoln, who is considered by many to be our nation's greatest president, lived and worked in Springfield.

(2007), have won great critical and commercial success. West is also a successful producer who has worked with artists including Alicia Keys, Jay-Z, and Janet Jackson.

Oprah Winfrey (1954–) Born in Mississippi in 1954, Winfrey became famous after she moved to Chicago and started her own talk show in 1984. Today, she is one of the most famous and wealthiest women in the world. Her media empire includes her talk show, *Oprah*; *O Magazine*; books; and Harpo Productions, which creates movies and television shows.

In 2008, Barack Obama made history when he was elected the first African American president of the United States.

Timeline

1000 BCE — 1600 CE	Native Americans build settlements in what is now Illinois.
1671	France claims the area that includes Illinois as part of its territory.
1673	Explorers Jacques Marquette and Louis Jolliet become the first Europeans to explore Illinois.
1754–1763	France and Great Britain fight the French and Indian War.
1763	Great Britain gains control of Illinois.
1779	Jean Baptiste Pointe du Sable builds a trading post that grows into the city of Chicago.
1818	Illinois becomes the twenty-first state.
1832	Americans defeat Chief Black Hawk and win the Black Hawk War, ending Native American claims on Illinois's land.
1837	Springfield becomes the capital of Illinois.
1848	The Illinois and Michigan Canal is completed, linking Lake Michigan in the east to the Mississippi River in the west.
1860	Illinois resident Abraham Lincoln is elected president of the United States.
1868	Illinois resident Ulysses S. Grant is elected president of the United States.
1871	The Great Chicago Fire destroys most of the city.
1893	Chicago hosts the World's Columbian Exposition.
1910	Large numbers of African Americans migrate to Illinois in search of jobs.
1942	The first nuclear reaction is created at a laboratory at the University of Chicago.
1980	Illinois native Ronald Reagan is elected president of the United States.
1986	Oprah Winfrey begins her Chicago-based television show.
1993	The Mississippi River floods millions of acres of Illinois farmland.
2008	Illinois resident Barack Obama becomes the first African American candidate from a major party to run for president and win the presidency.

Illinois at a Glance

State motto	"State Sovereignty, National Union"
State capital	Springfield
State flower	Purple violet
State bird	Cardinal
State tree	White oak
Statehood date and number	December 3, 1818; twenty-first state
State animal	White-tailed deer
State nickname	"Prairie State"
Total area and U.S. rank	57,915 square miles (149,999 sq km); twenty-fifth largest state
Approximate population at most recent census	12,419,293
Length of coastline	63 miles (101 km)
Highest and lowest elevations	Charles Mound, 1,235 feet (376 meters); Mississippi River, 279 feet (85 m)

ILLINOIS

State Flag

State Seal

Major rivers and lakes	Mississippi River, Illinois River, Lake Michigan
Hottest and coldest temperatures recorded and when	117 degrees Fahrenheit (47 degrees Celsius) at East St. Louis on July 14, 1954; -36°F (-38°C) at Congerville on January 5, 1999
Origin of state name	Illini Native American tribe
Major industries	Agriculture, manufacturing, mining, transportation, service
Chief agricultural products	Corn, soybeans, wheat, sorghum, hay, hogs, chickens, cattle, sheep
Chief industrial products	Food products, chemicals, machinery, transportation equipment, computer equipment, iron, steel, petroleum, coal
Border states	Indiana, Kentucky, Missouri, Iowa, Wisconsin, Michigan
Largest cities	Chicago, Aurora, Rockford, Naperville, Joliet, Springfield, Peoria
Geographic center	In Logan County, 28 miles (45 km) northeast of Springfield

State Bird

State Flower

agricultural Having to do with farming.

canals Channels dug across land to connect bodies of water.

candidate Someone who runs for a public office.

circuit courts Courts that operate on the local level.

confederation A union of several groups.

constitution Basic rules and laws that establish and run a government.

economy The earnings of an area, through the exchange of goods and services.

executive The group that runs a state or government.

exported Sent out of the country to another country to be sold.

federal Having to do with the national government.

fertile Good for growing plants.

glaciers Huge sheets of ice.

habitats Places where animals live.

immigrants People who leave one country to live in another country.

judicial Having to do with judges and courts.

legislature A group of people who make laws.

livestock Farm animals, such as pigs, cattle, sheep, and chickens.

migration The movement of a large group of people or animals from one place to another.

missionaries People who try to spread their religion to others.

prairie A large, mostly flat grassland with few trees.

resource Something valuable or useful.

settlers People who come to live in an area.

territory Land that is controlled by another nation.

treaty An official agreement between nations that ends a war.

FOR MORE INFORMATION

Abraham Lincoln Association
1 Old State Capitol Plaza
Springfield, IL 62701
(866) 865-8500
Web site: http://www.abrahamlincolnassociation.org
This organization is dedicated to the history of Abraham Lincoln and his achievements, and it sponsors many events and educational programs.

Chicago Convention and Tourism Board
2301 Lake Shore Drive
Chicago, IL 60616
(312) 567-8500
Web site: http://www.choosechicago.com
This organization provides information about tourist sites, transportation, restaurants, shopping, and other important Chicago facts.

Illinois Bureau of Tourism
620 East Adams Street
Springfield, IL 62701
(800) 2CONNECT
Web site: http://www.enjoyillinois.com
You will learn about the many interesting things to see and do in Illinois through this organization. Its Web site includes tourist information and photos.

Illinois State Historical Society
210 ½ South Sixth Street, Suite 200
Springfield, IL 62701
(217) 525-2781
Web site: http://www.historyillinois.org
Learn about Illinois's history from this state-sponsored organization.

Illinois State Museum
502 South Spring Street
Springfield, IL 62706
(217) 782-7386
Web site: http://www.museum.state.il.us
This organization runs several different state museums and features many different exhibits.

Web Sites

Due to the changing nature of Internet links, Rosen Publishing has developed an online list of Web sites related to the subject of this book. This site is updated regularly. Please use this link to access the list:

http://www.rosenlinks.com/uspp/ilpp

FOR FURTHER READING

Brill, Marlene Targ. *Illinois*. New York, NY: Benchmark Books, 2006.

Cisneros, Sandra. *The House on Mango Street*. New York, NY: Alfred A. Knopf, 1994.

Heinrichs, Ann. *Illinois*. Minneapolis, MN: Compass Point Books, 2003.

Hunt, Irene. *Across Five Aprils*. Morristown, NJ: Silver Burdett Press, 1993.

Marsh, Carole. *Illinois Geography Projects: 30 Cool Activities, Crafts, Experiments and More for Kids to Do*. Peachtree City, GA: Gallopade International, 2003.

Nobleman, Marc Tyler. *Chicago*. Milwaukee, WI: World Almanac Library, 2004.

Peck, Richard. *A Year Down Yonder*. New York, NY: Dial Books for Young Readers, 2000.

Price-Groff, Claire. *Illinois*. New York, NY: Marshall Cavendish, 2003.

Sievert, Terri. *Illinois: Land of Liberty*. Mankato, MN: Capstone Press, 2003.

Somervill, Barbara. *Illinois*. Brookfield, CT: Children's Press, 2008.

BIBLIOGRAPHY

Biles, Roger. *Illinois: A History of the Land and Its People*. DeKalb, IL: Northern Illinois University Press, 2005.

Burgan, Michael. *Illinois*. New York, NY: Children's Press, 2008.

Chicago Historical Society. "History Files: Chicago Fire." Retrieved November 15, 2008 (http://www.chicagohs.org/history/fire.html).

Fliege, Stu. *Tales and Trails of Illinois*. Champaign, IL: University of Illinois Press, 2002.

Illinois Department of Natural Resources. "Prairies of Illinois." Retrieved October 20, 2008 (http://dnr.state.il.us/conservation/naturalheritage/florafauna/document.htm).

Illinois Historic Preservation Agency. Retrieved October 20, 2008 (http://www.illinoishistory.gov/hs/sites.htm).

Illinois State Government Web Site. Retrieved October 20, 2008 (http://www.illinois.gov).

Illinois State Museum. "State Symbols." Retrieved October 20, 2008 (http://www.museum.state.il.us/exhibits/symbols).

Kay, Betty Carlson. *Illinois from A to Z*. Urbana, IL: University of Illinois Press, 2000.

Santella, Andrew. *People of Illinois*. Chicago, IL: Heinemann, 2003.

Schuldt, Lori Meek. *Fun with the Family in Illinois*. Augusta, GA: Globe Pequot, 2004.

Sorensen, Mark W. "The Illinois History Research Page." Retrieved October 20, 2008 (http://www.historyillinois.org/hist.html).

INDEX

About the Author

Joanne Mattern first visited Illinois while on a cross-country train trip. She enjoyed the beautiful countryside. A few years later, she spent time in Chicago, which has since become one of her favorite cities. She enjoys history, nature, travel, and discovering new places and interesting stories. She has written more than two hundred nonfiction books for children and works in her local library. Mattern lives in New York State with her husband, four children, and a menagerie of pets.

Photo Credits

Designer: Les Kanturek; Editor: Andrea Sclarow;
Photo Researcher: Cindy Reiman